S0-ARC-387

Fun and Silly Jokes For Kids and Family

500 Jokes That Will Tickle Your Funny Bone!

Riddleland

Table of Contents

Introduction

"Humor is the oxygen of children's literature. There's a lot of competition for children's, but even kids who hate to read want to a funny book." – Sid Fleischman

We would like to personally thank you for purchasing this book. **Fun and Silly for Kids and Family!** book is a collection of 500 fun and silly jokes that are written for children to develop their funny bone and also fall in love with reading!

These jokes are written to be fun and easy to read. Children learn best when they are playing. Reading can help increase that vocabulary and comprehension. They have also many other benefits such as:

- **Bonding** – It is an excellent way for parents and their children to spend some quality time and create some fun and memorable memories.

- **Confidence Building** - When parents give the riddles, it creates a safe environment for children to burst out answers even if they are incorrect. This helps the children to develop self confidence in expressing themselves.

- **Improve Vocabulary** – Riddles are usually written in advance words, therefore children will need to understand these words before they can share the riddles.

- **Better reading comprehension** – Many children can read at a young age but may not understand the context of the sentences. Jokes can help develop the children's interest to comprehend the context before they can share it to their friends.

- **Sense of humor** –Funny creative jokes can help children develop their sense of humor while getting their brains working.

Free Bonus – 50 Additional Funny Jokes and Stories

https://forms.aweber.com/form/93/463180293.htm

Thank you for buying this book, We would like to share a special bonus as a token of appreciation. It is collection 50 original jokes, riddles and 2 funny stories

RIDDLES AND JOKES CONTESTS!!

Riddleland is having **2 contests** to see who is the smartest or funniest boys and girls in the world!

1) **Creative and Challenging Riddles**
2) **Tickle Your Funny Bone Contest**

Parents, please email us your child's "Original" Riddle or Joke **and he or she could win a $50 gift card to Amazon.**

Here are the rules:

1) It must be challenging for the riddles and funny for the jokes!
2) It must be 100% Original and not something from the internet! It is easy to find out!
3) You can submit both joke and riddle as they are 2 separate contests.
4) No help from the parents unless they are as funny as you.
5) Winners will be announced via email.
6) Email us at Riddleland@bmccpublishing.com

Chapter 1: Knock! Knock! Who's There Jokes

1)   **Knock! Knock!**

Is there someone out there?

Wooden shoes!

Wooden shoes who?

Wooden shoes all laugh at this joke?

2)   **Ring! Ring!**

May I know who's on the other line?

Honeybee!

Honeybee who?

Honeybee a dear and open the door, please!

3) **Ding! Dong!**

Who's there?

Olive!

Olive who?

Olive you alone now.

4) **Buzz! Buzz!**

Someone at the door?

Turnip!

Oh yeah? Turnip who?

Turnip the volume to start the party!

5) **Brriing! Brriing!**

Tell me who's there!

Spell!

What? Spell who?

W-H-O

6)   **Ding! Dong!**

Is someone at the door?

It's **Cash!**

Yeah? Cash who?

No thanks, but I would love some almonds!

7)   **Knock! Knock!**

Hey! Who is there?

I'm **Barbie!**

Barbie who?

Barbie-Q flavored chips!

8)   **Chirp! Chirp!**

What's out there?

Closure!

Closure who?

Closure mouth when you are chewing!

9) **Bang! Bang!**

Who's at my door?

Donut!

Donut who?

Do-nut ask me, it's a secret!

10) **Knock! Knock!**

Hello – who is it?

Justin!

Justin who?

You are Justin time for the party!

11) **Brriing! Brriing!**

Who's speaking?

Tank!

Tank who?

Oh no, thank you very much for laughing at my joke!

12) **Ding! Dong!**

Who's at my door?

Luke!

Luke who?

Well, Luke at me and you'll know who I am!

13) **Knock! Knock!**

Who's there?

It's Etch!

Etch who?

What a sneeze! Bless you!

14) **Ring! Ring!**

Who's calling?

Cows go!

What? Cows go who?

That's ridiculous! Shouldn't cows MOO?

15) **Buzz! Buzz!**

Hey - who's there?

Who!

Who who?

Is there an owl in here?

16) **Chirp! Chirp!**

Who is calling, please?

Amish!

Amish who?

Aw, really? Well, I miss you too!

17) **Ring! Ring!**

Tell me, who's speaking?

Canoe!

Canoe who?

Canoe come outside with me to play?

18)   **Ding! Dong!**

Who's at my door?

My goat!

My goat who?

Do you think MY GOAT to joke is funny?

19)   **Knock! Knock!**

You have to tell me, who is there?

Two knee!

What? Two knee who?

Two knee fish tastes good, let's have lunch!

20)   **Beep! Beep!**

Is there someone there?

Lettuce!

Lettuce who?

Lettuce go now, we're late!

21) **Brriing! Brriing!**

Who's calling me now?

A broken yellow pencil!

A broken yellow pencil who?

Oh, never mind, there's just no point.

22) **Buzz! Buzz!**

Who's buzzin'?

It's Yukon!

Yeah? Yukon who?

Yukon not say a joke like mine!

23) **Ring! Ring!**

Who's calling?

Beets!

Beets who?

Beets me.

24) **Ring! Ring!**

Who is it?

I am!

I am who?

Haha! Did you forget your name?

25) **Beep! Beep!**

Who is beeping?

Double!

Double who?

W!

26) **Buzz! Buzz!**

Can you tell me what your name is?

It's Avenue!

Really? Avenue who?

This is quite an old joke. Avenue heard this one before?

27) Chirp! Chirp!

Who wants me now?

It's me, Loaf!

Loaf who?

You should be loaf-ing at this joke so much!

28) Bang! Bang!

Hold your horses - who's there?

It's Nana!

No kidding? Nana who?

Nana your beeswax!

29) Riiiing! Riiiing!

Is someone at my door?

Open up, it's Mikey!

Mikey who?

Come on, stop playing. I left Mikey, please open the door.

30) **Buzz! Buzz!**

May I know the name of the caller?

Cargo!

Cargo who?

Cargo beep beep!

31) **Brriing! Brriing!**

Who's ringing my bell?

It's Pecan!

What? Pecan? Pecan who?

Pecan someone your age!

32) **Chirp! Chirp!**

May I have your name?

Yah!

Yah who?

Are you a cowboy?

33)   **Buzz! Buzz!**

Who's buzzing my doorbell?

Hey, it's Figs!

Figs who?

You'll have to figs your doorbell. I've been knocking for too long!

34)   **Bang! Bang!**

Who's banging on my door?

Dishes!

Well - Dishes who?

Dishes the police. You have the right to remain silent!

35)   **Knock! Knock!**

Who is on the other side?

Wanda!

Wanda who?

Wanda come outside to play?

36) **Chirp! Chirp!**

Who's there?

It's Alpaca!

Really? Alpaca who?

Alpaca the suitcases, if you'll load the car!

37) **Ring! Ring!**

Sup?

It's Dwayne!

Yeah? Dwayne who?

Please Dwayne the bathtub, I'm dwowning!

38) **Ding! Dong!**

Who's there? Hey, who's there?

Someone who can't reach the doorbell!

39) **Buzz! Buzz!**

Who's calling?

Ho-Ho!

Yeah? Ho-Ho who?

Your imitation of Santa Clause needs some work.

40) **Knock! Knock!**

Who's knocking at my door?

Isabel!

Really, Isabel who?

Isabel broken? My knuckles hurt from knocking!

41) **Buzz! Buzz!**

Who is buzzing?

Noah!

Noah who?

Noah guy can better say this knock-knock joke?

42)   Bang! Bang!

Easy on the door - who's there?

It's Needle!

Uh, needle who?

I needle little bit more laughs for this joke!

43)   Knock! Knock!

Who is knocking?

You should know that it's me, it's Ketchup!

No. I'm sorry, Ketchup who?

Then, Ketchup with me and I'll tell you who!

44)   Ding! Dong!

Who's at the door?

Doris!

I am very sorry, Doris who?

Please open it! The Doris locked!

45) **Ring! Ring!**

Hello - who's calling?

Kanga!

Kanga who?

No, it's pronounced "Kangaroo!"

46) **Buzz! Buzz!**

Howdy - who's there?

You know, Howl!

I don't know anyone named Howl. Howl who?

Howl you know who I am if you don't see my face? Please open the door.

47) **Brriing! Brriing!**

Hello - may I know your name?

King Tut!

King Tut who?

I brought food! Do you want some King Tut-key fried chicken?

48) Knock! Knock!

Who's there?

Alex!

Who is Alex?

Alex-plain later!

49) Chirp! Chirp!

Who is on the other side?

A little old lady!

A little old lady who?

Wow, nice yodeling!

50) Ding! Dong!

So, who's there?

It's Europe!

No kidding? Europe who?

Not me, you're the poo!

51) **Bang! Bang!**

Hey – who is there?

Police!

What? Police who?

Police! Open this door. I need to get in, it's getting chilly now.

52) **Ring! Ring!**

Who's there?

My name is Otto!

Otto who?

Otto know. What are we talking about again?

53) **Buzz! Buzz!**

Who's buzzing?

Watson!

Watson who?

Watson T.V. tonight?

54)   **Brriing! Brriing!**

Hello - who's there?

Dewey!

Dewey who

Dewey still have joke coming? I'm running out!

55)   **Chirp! Chirp!**

Tell me, who's there?

Nose!

Nose who?

I nose so many good jokes!

56)   **Knock! Knock!**

Who's at the door?

It's me, Water!

I don't know you. Water who?

Water you doing coming into my house?

57)   **Ding! Dong!**

Who's ringing my bell?

Annie!

Annie who?

Annie body want to come outside to play?

58)   **Ring! Ring!**

Hey - who's there?

Hello – it's Eyesore!

What? Eyesore who?

Eyesore do love you! Bunches and bunches.

59)   **Buzz! Buzz!**

Who wants to come in?

A herd!

What? A herd who?

A herd this joke and I thought it's hilarious.

60) **Brriing! Brriing!**

Who's calling?

Me, Witches!

Who? Witches who?

Witches the road that goes to the park?

61) **Knock! Knock!**

Well - who's there?

You know me – it's Harry!

Nope, Harry who?

Harry up and let me in, it's snowing!

62) **Ding! Dong!**

Who wants in?

Hey, it's CD here!

CD who?

CD person on your doorstep? It's me!

63)   Ring! Ring!

Hi! Who's there?

Interrupting pirate!

Interrupting pi-

ARRRRRRRRRR!

64)   Chirp! Chirp!

Who's calling?

Hello! This is Stopwatch!

Stopwatch who?

Stopwatch-a doing right at this moment!

65)   Buzz! Buzz!

Hey - who's there?

Voodoo!

Voodoo who?

Voodoo you think knows the best jokes?

66)   **Ding! Dong!**

Who is there?

Hi! My name is Tinker Bell!

What? Tinker Bell who?

Tinker Bell does not work so I have to shout!

Please open the door!

67)   **Brriing! Brriing!**

Hi. Who's there?

It's a pile up!

That's crazy! A pile up who?

Ew! That's disgusting.

68)   **Riiiiiing!**

Who is ringing?

Abbot!

Abbot who?

Abbot you've never thought of this joke before!

69) **Buzz! Buzz!**

Hi - who's there?

You know - Howl!

No I don't - Howl who?

Howl I get you to go to the park with me?

70) **Chirp! Chirp!**

Howdy - who's there?

Icy!

Icy who?

Icy what you're doing!

71) **Ding! Dong!**

Who's at the door?

Ken!

Ken who?

Ken you make me some dinner?

72) **Buzz! Buzz!**

Who is calling me?

It's Viper!

Yeah? Viper who?

Viper snot! It is very disgusting!

73) **Knock! Knock!**

Who is it?

It's Seyz!

Seyz who?

Seyz me, that's who!

74) **Brriing! Brriing!**

Hi! Who's there?

Guitar!

Guitar who?

Guitar coat on and come play!

75)   **Buzz! Buzz!**

Hey, who's there?

Venice!

Venice who?

Venice dinner going to be ready?

76)   **Knock! Knock!**

Who's knocking at my door?

Hi! It's Gorilla!

Oh yeah? Gorilla who?

Gorilla up some burgers, I'm starving!

77)   **Ding! Dong!**

Who's at my door?

Iran!

Iran who?

Iran all the way here, let me in!

78) **Ring! Ring!**

Who's calling?

Amos!

Amos who?

***clap your hands* I caught Amos-quito!**

79) **Knock! Knock!**

Who is it?

Howdy! It's Moustache!

Moustache who?

I moustache you an important question, but I can shave it for later.

80) **Brriing! Brriing!**

Hi, who's there?

It's Toucan!

What? Toucan who?

Well, Toucan play at this game!

81) **Buzz! Buzz!**

Hello. Who's at my door?

Adore!

I don't know anyone named Adore? Who are you?

We can't hear each other! Adore is between us!

Please open it!

82) **Ding! Dong!**

Who's at my door?

Ice cream soda!

Really? Ice cream soda who?

Ice cream soda you can hear me! Come closer!

83) **Brriing! Brriing!**

Howdy, who's there?

Honeydew speaking!

Honeydew who?

Honeydew you deliver this joke better?

84)   Knock! Knock!

What is your name?

Icon!

Icon who?

Icon tell more jokes than you can!

85)   Chirp! Chirp!

Tell me who's there?

Pea!

Pea who?

Pea who! What stinks so bad?

86)   Buzz! Buzz!

Who's calling?

To!

To who?

No, it's "to whom."

87) Ding! Dong!

Who's at my door?

Norway!

Norway who?

Norway I'm leaving, so open up!

88) Ring! Ring!

Who's there?

It's Wire!

What? Wire who?

Wire you always asking me "who's there?"

89) Buuuzzzz!!!

Hi! Is someone there?

You know - Frank!

Nope. Frank who?

Frank you for being so kind to me.

90) **Ding! Dong!**

Who's on my porch?

Tokyo!

Tokyo who?

What Tokyo so long to open the door?

91) **Bang! Bang!**

Geez - who's there?

Ivy!

Ivy who?

Ivy sore wrist from knocking so long!

92) **Ring! Ring!**

Hello. Who's there?

Kenya!

Kenya who?

Kenya come out and play?

93) **Buzz! Buzz!**

Who is it?

I love!

I love, who?

Did you forget who you love?

94) **Ding! Dong!**

May I please know who is there?

I did up!

I did up who?

Eww! You did a poo?!

95) **Brriing! Brriing!**

Howdy! Who's there?

It's Anita!

Yeah? Anita who?

Anita borrow some sugar!

96)   **Ding! Dong!**

Hey - who's there?

Carrot!

Carrot who?

Carrot-e chop!

97)   **Bang! Bang!**

Who's at my door?

Good evening, it's Broccoli!

Do I know you? Broccoli who?

Broccoli doesn't have the last name, silly!

98)   **Ring! Ring!**

Who's calling?

Claire!

Claire who?

Claire the way, I'm coming in!

99) **Buzz! Buzz!**

Who is it?

It's Althea!

What? Althea who?

Althea later, alligator!

100) **Brriing! Brriing!**

What - who's there?

Shelby!

Shelby who?

Shelby coming around the mountain when she comes!

101) **Ding! Dong!**

Who's at my door?

Mary and Abby!

Mary and Abby who?

Mary Christmas and Abby New Year!

102) **Bang! Bang!**

Who's there?

A knee!

A knee who?

A knee one you like!

103) **Buzz! Buzz!**

Who's calling?

Grab!

Grab who?

Not me!

104) **Ring! Ring!**

Hi. Who's there?

Hey you! It's Butter!

I don't know who butter is. Butter who?

Then, I think, I butter not tell you!

105)   **Brriing! Brriing!**

Hello. Who is it?

You know me - Value!

No I don't. Value who?

Value be my friend?

106)   **Knock! Knock!**

Who's there?

Yorkies!

Yorkies who?

I think you should knock instead, yorkies don't fit the lock!

107)   **Buzz! Buzz!**

Who's at my door?

Hey, it's Roach!

I am sorry, Roach who?

Roach you quite a long letter. Were you able to get it?

108) **Ring! Ring!**

Who is it?

The polite interrupting cow!

The polite inter-

Excuse me, I'm sorry to interrupt, but MOO!

109) **Chirp! Chirp!**

Hi. Who's there?

Hawaii!

Hawaii who?

Why thank you! I am very good, Hawaii you?

110) **Brriing! Brriing!**

Howdy. Who's there?

Owl!

Owl who?

Owl aboard, the train's leaving!

111) **Bang! Bang!**

Who's at the door?

Aardvark!

Aardvark who?

Aardvark a hundred miles to see you!

112) **Knock! Knock!**

Who is it?

It's Scold!

What? Scold who?

It's Scold enough to go ice fishing out here!

113) **Ring! Ring!**

Who's calling?

I'm Oswald!

You are Oswald? Oswald who?

Oh no! Oswald my bubble gum!

114) **Buzz! Buzz!**

Who's at the door?

Gopher!

Gopher who?

I could gopher a cup of hot chocolate right now!

115) **Chirp! Chirp!**

Hi. Who's there?

Berry!

Berry who?

Berry nice to see you!

116) **Brriing! Brriing!**

Hello -who is it?

It's Howard!

Yeah? Howard who?

Howard I know?

117) **Bang! Bang!**

Who's at the door?

Rhino!

Rhino who?

Rhino all the best jokes!

118) **Ding! Dong!**

Who ringing my bell there?

Repeat!

I'm terribly sorry. Repeat who?

Who?

119) **Buzz! Buzz!**

May I know who is calling?

Iguana!

Iguana who?

Iguana be your friend!

120) **Chirp! Chirp!**

Hey - who's there?

Panther!

Panther who?

I forgot my belt, so my panther falling down!

121) **Bang! Bang!**

Who's on my porch?

Sore ewe!

Sore ewe who?

Sore ewe going to open the door or not?

122) **Ring! Ring!**

Hey - who's calling?

Alaska!

Alaska who?

Alaska the teacher if she knows the answer!

123)   Knock! Knock!

So, who is it?

Open up for Aida!

No way - Aida who?

Aida lot of cookies, now my tummy hurts!

124)   Brriing! Brriing!

Howdy. Who's calling?

It's Heart!

What? Heart who?

It's Heart to hear you! You have to speak loudly!

125) **Buzz! Buzz!**

Who's there?

Banana!

Banana who?

Buzz! Buzz!

Who's there?

Banana!

Banana who?

Buzz! Buzz!

Who's there?

Orange!

Orange who?

Orange you glad I didn't say "banana?"

Chapter 2 - Animal Jokes

1) **Why are leopards terrible at hide and seek?**

Because they're always spotted!

2) **Cross an elephant with a potato – what do you get?**

Mashed potatoes!

3) **My pretty kitten Princess won the dog show? Do you know what my Dad said?**

It was a total cat-has-trophy!

4) **Why are elephants such bad dancers?**

Because they have two left feet!

5) **What do you get when you combine a cat with a parrot?**

A carrot!

6) **What's the best thing you can do if an elephant sneezes?**

Get out of its way!

7) **Why did the dog turn on the air conditioner?**

She was a hot dog!

8) **What happens when elephants get lightheaded?**

They ele-faint!

9) **What do you give an elephant with big feet?**

Plenty of room!

10) **What do elephants do at night?**

Watch ele-vision.

**11)	You wake up to find an elephant sitting on our bed. What time is it?**

Time to get a new bed!

**12)	What do you get if you cross an elephant with a fish?**

You get swimming trunks!

**13)	What weighs over 4,000 pounds and looks beautiful in glass slippers?**

Cinderellephant!

**14)	Do you know the best way to keep a bull elephant from scary charging?**

Take away all its credit cards!

**15)	Name the cat's favorite color?**

Purrrr-ple!

16)   Why are elephants so wrinkled?

Because they don't fit on an ironing board!

17)   Why do elephants never forget?

Because nobody ever tells them anything!

18)   How does a cat stop a movie on DVD?

By pressing the "paws" button!

19)   What is a cat's favorite movie?

The Sound of Meow-sic!

20)   Where do the school kittens go for their field trip?

The Meow-seum!

21)   How do you know your cat used the computer?

The mouse has teeth marks on it!

22)   Why did the cat go to medical school?

To become a First-Aid Kit!

23)   How do cats eat pasta?

With their mouths, just like everyone else!

24)   How is a cat like a coin?

It has a head on one side and a tail on the other!

25)   What do you get when you cross a cat and a shark?

A catfish!

26)   What type of a cat like to go bowling?

An alley cat!

27)   What does a cat say when somebody steps on its tail?

Me-OWWW!

28)   What state has a lot of cats and dogs?

Petsylvania

29)   What do cats wear when they sleep?

Paw-jamas!

30)   Why are cats bad storytellers?

Because they only have one tail!

31)   If you see a blue elephant, what should you do?

Try to cheer it up!

32)   Which dog breed will always laugh at your jokes?

A Chi-ha-ha!

33)   What's a dog's favorite dessert?

Pupcakes!

34) **What is the term for an elephant in a telephone box?**

Stuck!

35) **What happens when you cross a dog with a phone?**

You get a Golden Receiver!

36) **Do you know why the dog crossed the road twice?**

It was trying to fetch a boomerang!

37) **What kind of dog keeps the best time?**

A watchdog!

38) **What are bears with no ears?**

B!

39) **Which kind of dogs loves bubble baths?**

Sham-poodles!

40) **What do you call a dog playing in the snow?**

A chilly dog!

41) **What do you call the greatest doggie detective?**

Mr. Sherlock Bones!

42) **What did the waiter say when he brought the dog its food?**

Bone appétit!

43) **What is a dog's favorite place to shop?**

A re-tail store!

44) **What is a dog's least favorite place to shop?**

A flea market!

45) **What do you get when you mix a tulip with a sheepdog?**

A collie-flower!

46)   What is a dog's favorite type of pizza?

Pupperoni!

47)   How do camels hide?

They put on camel-flage!

48)   What is a horse's favorite game?

Stable tennis!

49)   What do cows love to play at parties?

Moo-sical chairs!

50)   What is a fish with no eyes?

A f-sh!

51)   What kind of fish only swims at night?

A starfish!

52) **What did the dog say to the flea?**

Stop bugging me!

53) **What's a pig's favorite place to go on vacation?**

Ham-sterdam!

54) **What would you call an alligator detective?**

An investi-gator!

55) **What do you call a fly who doesn't have any wings?**

A walk!

56) **Where do cows like to go with their friends?**

To the moo-vies!

57) **After a bath, how does a mouse feel?**

Squeaky clean!

58)   What do you call it when a hippopotamus doesn't clean its room?

A hippopota-mess!

59)   What did the cow say when its friend was walking too slow?

Moo-ve faster!

60)   What animal can be heard to say oom?

A cow that is walking backward!

61)   Where do dogs put their cars?

In a barking lot!

62)   What kind of key can't open a door?

A turkey!

63)   Where do fish save their money?

A riverbank!

64) **What is the strongest animal?**

A snail because it carries its house on its back!

65) **I saw a bear in the woods but I wasn't afraid because when he growled at me, he had no teeth. Why not?**

He was a gummy bear!

66) **How did the chicken get very strong?**

It egg-cersized!

67) **Why did the farmer put bells on all the cows?**

Because their horns didn't honk!

68) **What happens when you mix a porcupine and a balloon?**

POP!

69)   What is a pig who practices karate?

A pork-chop!

70)   What do you call a bunch of ducks in a container?

A box of quackers!

71)   How did the farmer count his cattle?

He used a cow-culator!

72)   What happened to the lion when he ate a clown?

He felt funny!

73)   An earthquake hits San Francisco. What do you call the cow on a nearby farm?

A milkshake!

74)   What do you give a bird when it gets sick?

A tweetment!

75)   **How do you stop a skunk from smelling?**

Plug its nose!

76)   **This creature is smarter than a talking parrot –**

what is it?

A spelling bee!

77)   **On a ride to the vet, my dog starts barking in the**

back seat. How do I get him to stop?

Put him in the front seat!

78)   **What do you call a monkey wearing earplugs?**

Don't worry, whatever you call him, he still cannot hear you!

79)   **What is a snake who works as a baker?**

A pie-thon!

80) **What happened when the monkey chased the banana?**

The banana split!

81) **What is the best treatment for a pig who has a rash?**

Oinkment!

82) **How many tickles are necessary to make an octopus laugh?**

Ten-tickles!

83) **What did the Cinderella fish wear to the ball?**

Glass flippers!

84) **Why did the policeman give the sheep a ticket?**

He was a baaad driver!

85) **What's white and black and red all over?**

A zebra that has a sunburn!

86) **What do you call an elephant throwing a tantrum?**

An earthquake!

87) **What is a knight's favorite fish?**

A swordfish!

88) **What is a dog's favorite year?**

Leap year!

89) **Where do horses live?**

In a neigh-borhood!

90) **What is the term for a cow with a shudder?**

Beef jerky!

91) **What kind of shoes does a bear wear?**

None, they prefer bear feet!

92) **What kind of dinosaur loves to take naps?**

A stega-snore-us!

93) **Why do fish prefer saltwater?**

Because pepper water would make them sneeze.

94) **Why couldn't the Polly the Pony sing the national anthem?**

Because she was a little hoarse.

95) **What do you call a dinosaur who doesn't give up?**

A try-ceratops!

96) **What has six eyes but cannot see?**

Three blind mice!

97) **Where did the three blind mice park their boats?**

Down at the hickory dickory dock, of course!

98) **What is a snake's favorite subject in school?**

Hiss-tory!

99) **What type of soda is a frog's favorite soda?**

Croak-a-cola!

100) **Why does a dog wag its tail?**

Because no one else can wag it for him!

101) **How do you make a goldfish old?**

Take away the "g!"

102) **Where does a lamb get a haircut?**

At the baabaa shop!

103) **Where do elephants put their luggage when they go on vacation?**

In their trunks!

104) **What is a frog's favorite food?**

French Flies!

105) **What is a cat's favorite type of car?**

A cat-illac!

106) **There were three cats in a boat. One jumped out. How many cats stayed in the boat?**

None, they were all copycats!

107) **What is a cheetah's favorite kind of food?**

Fast food!

108) **What do you call a deer that costs a dollar?**

A buck!

109) Where can you locate a chicken that doesn't have legs?

Wherever you left it!

110) What is a dog's favorite breakfast food?

Pooched eggs!

111) Why is a frog like a baseball player?

They both catch flies!

112) Why wasn't the female butterfly allowed into the school dance?

Because it was a moth ball!

113) What letter hurts if you get too close to it?

A bee!

114) **Why did the tired kangaroo get a penalty in the football game?**

It was out of bounds!

115) **What do you do if your dog swallows your pencil?**

Use a pen!

116) **What did the carrot say to the rabbit?**

Want to grab a bite?

117) **Why did the fly, fly?**

Because the spider spied her!

118) **When the skunk walked into the courtroom, what did the judge say?**

"Odor in the court!"

119) **What does a puppy become on its second birthday?**

Two years old!

120) **What do you call a cold puppy sitting on a rabbit?**

A chili dog on a bun!

121) **What do you call a snail on a ship?**

A snailor!

122) **Where does a polar bear go to vote?**

The North Poll!

123) **What does the octopus wear when it gets cold?**

A coat of arms!

124) **What do you call a Stegosaurus mixed with the farmer's pig?**

Jurassic pork!

125) What do you call a cow without a map?

Udderly lost!

126) What did the firefly say to her sister firefly?

You glow girl!

127) What do you call a bull that is snoring?

A bull-dozer

128) What did the male bee say to the female bee?

You sting girl!

Chapter 3 - Wordplay Jokes

1) **My baby brother threw the butter out the kitchen window - why?**

He wanted to see a butterfly!

2) **The Boy Scout buried his flashlight. Why?**

The batteries died!

3) **Which letter of the alphabet has the most water?**

C!

4) **If everyone bought a white car, what would we have?**

A white carnation!

5) **Where can a chef learn to make banana splits?**

In sundae school!

6) **A man is lying on your doorstep. What is his name?**

Matt!

7) **Did you hear about the actor who broke through the floorboards?**

He was just going through a stage!

8) **Why are my favorite unicorn never hungry?**

Why, because they're stuffed, of course!

9) **Why did the banana visit a doctor?**

It wasn't peeling very well.

10) **What happens when you cross a vampire with a snowman?**

Frostbite!

11)   **Why did the melon jump into the pool?**

It wanted to be a watermelon!

12)   **What is crimson red and smells just like blue**

paint?

Red paint!

13)   **Would you like to hear a pizza joke?**

Never mind, it's just too cheesy!

14)   **Why did the burglar rob a bakery?**

Because he needed the dough!

15)   **Your left eye is talking to your right eye while you**

sleep.

What did it say?

Hey - between us, something smells!

16)   **Why did the oatmeal cookie visit to the doctor?**

It was feeling crumb-y!

17)   **What's a twelve inches long and slippery?**

A slipper!

18)   **Why isn't Jack the fishermen generous?**

Because selling lobster makes him sell fish!

19)   **How do you make fire with two sticks?**

Make sure one is a match!

20)   **What did the generous plate say to his friend the saucer?**

Dinner is on me!

21)   **What do you call gooey plate of cheese that isn't yours?**

Nacho cheese!

22) **The burglar took a shower in the middle of breaking into a house - why?**

He wanted a clean getaway!

23) **Do you know about Paul? His entire left body was paralyzed!**

It's OK, he's all right now!

24) **Why did the belt go to prison?**

It was arrested for holding up a pair of pants!

25) **How do you stop an astronaut's baby from crying?**

You rocket!

26) **What do you call it when you help a lemon that's in trouble?**

Lemon-aid!

27) **Which way works best for the man in the moon to cut the hair in his ears?**

Eclipse it!

28) **Where do burgers like to dance?**

A meatball!

29) **What is a witch's favorite subject in school?**

Spelling!

30) **What do elves learn at school?**

The elf-abet!

31) **What's faster: low temperatures or high?**

Hot, because you can catch a cold!

32) **Why don't ducks ever have any spare change?**

They only carry bills!

33) How do you make a lemon drop?

Just let it fall!

34) Why was the Geometry book depressed?

Because it had so many problems!

35) Why wouldn't the blue crab share his red candy?

He was just too shellfish to share!

36) Mark ate his math homework for lunch. Why?

Because his teacher told him it would be a piece of cake!

37) Why does a seagull only take flight over the sea?

Because if it flew over the bay, it would be a "bay-gull!"

38) What did the calculator say to the student?

You can count on me!

39) **Why did the soprano opera singer go on a cruise?**

She wanted to hit the high C's!

40) **What do rabbits do when they get married?**

Go on a bunnymoon!

41) **What species of tree is possible to carry in your hand?**

A palm tree!

42) **Brandon is in seventh grade and when his Mom opens his report card, it's all wet – why?**

It was below C level!

43) **What is a synonym for "fake noodle?"**

An impasta!

44) **What kind of table can you eat?**

A vege-table!

45)   **How do you talk to a giant?**

Use big words!

46)   **What does the Oceans often say to the Seas?**

Not one thing, oceans can't talk, but they always wave!

47)   **What is a librarian's favorite kind of vegetable?**

Quiet peas!

48)   **What is it that you call two banana peels?**

A pair of slippers!

49)   **What did the girl volcano whisper to the boy volcano?**

I lava you!

50)   **What's the worst thing about throwing a party in space?**

You have to planet!

51) **Why did the physicist install a big brass knocker on her door?**

She wanted to win the no-bell prize!

52) **How do you mend a broken orange squash?**

With a pumpkin patch!

53) **Why did Jason put all of his money into his freezer?**

He wanted stacks of cold hard cash!

54) **Why do people always laugh at the mountains?**

Because they're hill areas!

55) **What do ninjas eat for lunch?**

Kung-food!

56)   **What did one nut say when it was chasing the other nut?**

I'm going to cashew!

57)   **What dinosaur had the best vocabulary?**

The Thesaurus!

58)   **What kind of music do planets listen to?**

Nep-tunes!

59)   **What do you call a snake on a building site?**

A boa constructor!

60)   **Why did the boy take a ruler to bed with him?**

To see how long he slept!

61)   **Why didn't the orange win the race?**

It ran out of juice!

62)   **What washes up on very small beaches?**

Micro-waves!

63)   **What would you find on the ocean floor, worrying or distressed?**

A nervous wreck!

64)   **Carson is an astronaut. When does he eat?**

At launch time!

65)   **What do you call an old snowman?**

A puddle!

66)   **When do you know the moon has had enough to eat?**

When it's full!

67)   **What are the strongest creatures in the ocean?**

Mussels!

68) **What did the front wall say to the side wall?**

Hey baby - I'll meet you at the corner!

69) **Why did the maple tree go to visit the dentist?**

It had to have a root canal!

70) **What did one copper penny say to the other copper penny?**

We make cents!

71) **Why do they eat snails in France?**

They don't like fast food!

72) **Which creature can jump higher than a two-story house?**

Any creature! Houses can't jump!

73) **What did the big flower say to the little flower?**

Hi, bud!

74)   What did the comforter say to the mattress?

No sweat! I've got you covered!

75)   What did the envelope say to the postage stamp?

If you stick with me, we can really go places!

76)   Why was the gymnasium so stuffy and hot after the basketball game?

Because all of the fans left!

77)   What kind of award did the dentist receive?

A little plaque!

78)   Why didn't the scary skeleton go to the fancy dance?

He had no body to dance with!

79)   Why did the drum take a nap?

It was beat!

80) **Why hasn't anyone's nose ever measured twelve inches long?**

Because then it would be a foot!

81) **Why did Frank, who coached football, go to the credit union?**

To get his quarterback!

82) **What do you call a dog magician?**

A labracadabrador!

83) **What type of footwear do spies wear?**

Sneakers!

84) **How does the forest connect to the internet?**

It logs in!

85) **What kind of musical instrument can you find in your bathroom?**

A tuba toothpaste!

86) **What is a Candy the cheerleader's favorite drink?**

Root beer!

87) **Why did the leaf go to the doctor?**

His upset stomach made him feel a bit green!

88) **What did your nose say to your finger?**

Quit picking on me!

89) **What's brown and sticky?**

A stick!

90) **Why did the professional golfer wear two layers of shorts on the golf course?**

In case he got a hole in one!

91)   What happens when you tell a joke to an egg?

It cracks up!

92)   What is the easiest way to make a tissue dance?

You put a little boogie in it!

93)   Why did the policeman go to the baseball game?

He heard that someone had stolen a base!

94)   Why wouldn't the bicycle stand up?

It was two tired!

95)   What do you get when a rabbit sits on your head?

A bad hare day!

96)   What kind of sandals do frogs wear?

Open toad!

97)   **You are sitting on the couch when the clock strikes 13. What time is it?**

Time to get a new clock!

98)   **Why was Humpty Dumpty happiest in October?**

Because Humpty Dumpty had a great Fall!

99)   **What did the avocado say to the dog?**

What? Nothing since avocados can't talk!

100)   **What do computers eat for a snack?**

Microchips!

101)   **What is a tornado's favorite game to play?**

Twister!

102)   **Why can't you trust an atom?**

Because they make up everything!

103) How does a scientist freshen her breath?

With experi-mints!

104) What is the building towers over the entire world?

The library, because it has so many stories!

105) How much money does it cost for a pirate to get his ears pierced?

About a buck an ear!

106) Why did my baby brother throw his clock out his bedroom window?

He wanted to see how time flies!

107) Why is it that Peter Pan is always flying?

Because he never-lands!

108) **What do you call a person without a nose or a body?**

Nobodynose!

109) **Why did the farmer give the scarecrow a promotion?**

He had to since scarecrow has really been outstanding in his field!

110) **What is a belt that has a watch on it?**

A waist of time!

111) **Why are hairdressers never late for work?**

Because they know all the short cuts!

112) **What do you do with a sick boat?**

Take it to the doc!

113)   **Why did the painting go to jail?**

It was framed!

114)   **What is the color of the wind?**

Blew!

115)   **Why did the black widow buy a laptop?**

To make a web-site!

116)   **What did the Bob, the beaver, whisper to its first**

pine tree?

It's been nice gnawing you!

117)   **How do you make a witch itch?**

Take away her "w!"

118)   **What do cars eat on their toast?**

Traffic jam!

119)   Why did the pirate have trouble learning the alphabet?

Because he always got lost at "c!"

120)   What do eggs do for fun?

Sing kara-yolk-e!

121)   Did I ever tell you the story of the magic sandwich?

Never mind, it's just a bunch of bologna.

122)   I've been snail racing and he lost. So, for the next race, I took the shell off to try to make him faster, but....

It just made him sluggish.

123)   My new hobby is eating clocks.

It's rather time-consuming.

124) I was out in left field waiting when I pondered why the baseball was growing.

Then it hit me.

125) Two hats were talking while they were dangling on a hook at my entryway.

One had to go and whispered to the other, "You stay here, I'll go on a head."

128) When I woke up today, I forgot which side the sun rises on.

Then it dawned on me.

129) My dog can do some crazy magic tricks.

He's a special breed - a l-abracadabra-dor.

131) I found a lion in my closet and when I asked him what he was doing there?

He said it was "Narnia Business."

132) My friend made a stupid joke about his Dad's fancy TV controller.

But it wasn't remotely funny.

133) I went to my favorite restaurant last night and ordered something called the Wookie steak

I liked it, but it was a little chewy.

134) When you sing during your shower, it's all good clean fun until you get shampoo suds in your mouth

Then suddenly it's a soap opera.

135) I'm glad my Mom taught me sign language.

It comes in pretty handy.

136) My best friend's Mom owns a bakery, but it burned down last night.

Looks like her business is toast.

137)   When the lion arrived late for dinner.

All the others gave him the cold shoulder.

138)   Yesterday in my kitchen, I swallowed some food coloring by accident.

My pediatrician says I'll be fine, but I feel a little blue.

139)   Did you hear the story about Dan, who got was struck in the head with a can of soda in the park?

Dan was sure lucky it was a soft drink.

138)   I used to be afraid of running the hurdles, but I got over it.

139)   I replaced my Mom's bed with a trampoline.

She was so mad, she hit the roof.

141)   I tried to catch some fog but I mist.

142)   Did you know **taller** people sleep **longer** in bed?

143)   Puns about **cockroaches** just **bug** me.

144)   I'm very close with only 25 letters of the alphabet. I don't know why.

145) Being employed to inspect mirrors sounds like a cool job and is something. I could really see **myself** doing.

Chapter 4 – Riddles Jokes

1)   **What is light as a feather but as big as an elephant?**

An elephant's shadow!

2)   **What is 100 feet in the air while it's lying on the ground?**

A centipede on its back!

3)   **What five letter word becomes shorter by adding just two letters?**

Short!

4)   **What has no arms, no legs, but a face and two hands?**

The face of a clock!

5) **What gets wet while it's drying?**

A towel!

6) **What sleeps through the day and cries through the night, and the more it cries, the more it creates light?**

A candle!

7) **What begins with an "e" and ends with "e" and contains only one letter?**

An envelope!

8) **What uses its ear to speak and its mouth to hear?**

A telephone!

9) **How many months of the year have 28 days?**

All of them!

10) **What must be damaged before you can use it?**

An egg!

11) **What goes down but can never go up?**

Rain!

12) **What goes up and up but can never go down?**

Your age!

13) **What has teeth but cannot chew?**

A comb!

15) **It starts with a T, is filled with T, and ends with T too. What is it?**

A teapot!

16) **Stars with "p", ends with "e", and contains thousands of letters?**

Post Office!

17) **Why would a man who is living in New York not be allowed to be buried in Chicago?**

Because he is still alive!

18) **What number goes away when you add the letter "g"?**

One! If you add the letter "g" to one, then it's gone!

19) **What two things can you never be eaten just for breakfast?**

Only dinner or lunch!

20) **This can be broken without being touched. What is it?**

A promise!

21) **Three men were in a boat. It capsized, but on two men got their hair wet. Why?**

One of the men was bald!

22)   I like food, but water kills me. What am I?

Fire!

23)   Everyone has me, and no one can lose me. What

am I?

A shadow!

24)   Where is it possible for Friday to come before

Thursday?

In the dictionary!

25)   What has one eye, but cannot see?

A needle!

26)   I am hard like a stone, but I grow on your body.

What am I?

A tooth!

27) **A rodeo clown rides into a new town on Tuesday, stays five whole days, and then leaves on Tuesday. How?**

His horse is named Tuesday!

28) **Mary's parents have five daughters. Four of the daughters are named Nana, Nini, Nono, and Nene. What is the name of the fifth daughter?**

Mary!

29) **What stays in place when it goes off?**

An alarm clock!

30) **You can't come in or go out without me. What am I?**

A door!

31) **What is so fragile and delicate that uttering its name can break it?**

Silence!

32) **What needs an answer but doesn't ask any questions?**

A telephone!

33) **I'm excellent to taste but horrible to smell. What am I?**

A tongue!

34) **What has ears but cannot hear?**

A cornfield!

35) **I stay in one corner but go the whole way around the world. What am I?**

A stamp!

36)   **What falls in winter but never gets hurt?**

Snow!

37)   **What kind of a button cannot be unbuttoned?**

A bellybutton!

38)   **What has a bed, but doesn't sleep, and has a mouth, but never speaks?**

A river!

39)   **What occurs only one time in a minute, then twice in one moment, but never at all in a whole decade?**

The letter "m."

40)   **What runs around a yard without actually moving?**

A fence!

41) **What is as weightless as down, but even the biggest, strongest man in the world can't hold it very long?**

Breath!

42) **I have many keys but yet no doors, and big space but no rooms. I will allow you to enter, and you can escape if you want, but you can't exit. What am I?**

A keyboard!

43) **What word is spelled wrong in all the dictionaries?**

Wrong!

44) **What kind of lion never roars?**

A dande-lion!

45) If you picked up a stone and threw it into the Red Sea, what would it become?

Wet!

46) What has wings and is able to fly, is not a bird, but soars high in the sky?

An airplane!

47) The more you leave me behind, the more you take of me. What am I?

Footsteps!

48) The more you have of it, the less you see. What is it?

Darkness!

49) What has many rings, but no fingers?

A telephone!

50) **Which one weighs more, a pound of tissues or a pound of textbooks?**

Neither one, they both weigh one pound!

51) **What grows even bigger the more you take away from it?**

A hole!

52) **If a car key would open a car, and a house key would open a house, then what would open a banana?**

A monkey!

53) **What can be held without ever being touched?**

A conversation!

54) **How is it possible to make seven even?**

Take away the "s!"

55) **What has four legs, but one foot, and just one head?**

A bed!

56) **What can you not keep until you give it?**

Your word!

57) **What can go through Nashville and over the Great Smoky Mountains but yet never move?**

A road!

58) **What invention allows you to see through a wall?**

A window!

59) **What can't you see that is always ahead of you?**

The future!

60) **What belongs to you, but is used mostly by others?**

Your name!

61) **What word has five letters, but sounds like it only has one?**

Queue!

62) **What object is jam-packed of holes, but yet can still hold water?**

A sponge!

63) **What has four legs, but still can't walk?**

A table!

64) **How much dirt is in a hole that is 6 feet wide and 9 feet deep?**

None!

65) **I sound like one letter but am written with three, and I show you things when you look through me. What am I?**

An eye!

66) **What was the first planet discovered by humans?**

Earth!

67) **What kind of room doesn't have a door or a window?**

A mushroom!

68) **I have a lot of keys, but I cannot unlock a single door. What am I?**

A piano, of course!

69) **What can run but can't walk?**

Water!

70) **If I have it, then I do not share it. But if I do share it, then I do not actually have it. What is it?**

A secret!

71) **What can you make that you can't see?**

Noise!

72) **People will go to the store and buy me in order to eat, but will never eat me. What am I?**

A plate!

73) **What do cats, dogs, birds, fish, and turtles all have in common?**

The letter "S"!

74) **I can help you from your head to your toes. But, the more I work, the smaller I grow. What am I?**

A bar of soap!

75)   **What misses its head after the morning, but gains it back later that night?**

A pillow!

76)   **What goes up to the sky when the rain comes down to the ground?**

An umbrella!

77)   **Black when it's clean and white when it's dirty – what is it?**

A blackboard!

78)   **You can certainly catch me, but can't ever throw me. What am I?**

A cold!

79)   **What flies around all day, but never goes anywhere?**

A flag!

80) **What has feet on the inside, but not on the outside?**

Shoes!

81) **What is made of water, but if you put it into water it will disappear?**

An ice cube!

82) **I am an instrument through which sounds are made, but I am not something that can be played. What am I?**

Your voice!

83) **What kind of dress can never be worn?**

An address!

84) **What has a neck but yet no head, and still wears a cap?**

A bottle!

85)   **What always sleeps with its shoes on?**

A horse!

86)   **I am hard to get out of, but easy to get into. What am I?**

Trouble!

87)   **You can serve it but never eat it. What is it?**

A ball!

88)   **What can go through glass without breaking it?**

Light!

89)   **What has four eyes, but cannot see?**

Mississippi!

90)   **What can honk without a horn?**

A goose!

91)   **What has a horn but cannot honk?**

A Rhinoceros!

92)   **What kind of bet can never be won?**

The alphabet!

93)   **My head is red, but turns black if you scratch it.**

What am I?

A match!

94)   **I clap, but I don't have any hands. What am I?**

Thunder!

95)   **You'll see me up in the sky without wings and**

shedding tears without eyes. What am I?

A cloud!

96) **You can find me in the past, you can make me in the present, but the future can never change me. What am I?**

History!

97) **What has a bark, but no bite?**

A tree!

98) **My pet cat is named Princess. What does a Princess have that no other animal has?**

Kittens!

99) **What wears a jacket, but no pants?**

A book!

100) **You can look me in eyes in the water, but I will never be wet. What am I?**

A reflection!

101) **I always tell the truth, but can neither speak nor hear. What am I?**

A mirror!

102) **People without money already have it, people with lots of money want it, and if you only eat it, you will die. What is it?**

Nothing!

103) **I am a ball that can be rolled, but never bounced or thrown. What am I?**

An eyeball!

104) **What goes down and up, but never, ever moves?**

A flight of stairs!

105) **I can be liquid or solid, sometimes I bubble, and you can find me in every home. What am I?**

Soap!

106) How many seconds are there in February?

Just one, February 2nd!

107) Warning: railroad crossing. Look out for stopped cars. Can you spell that without the letter "R?"

T-H-A-T!

108) Do you know the number of apples that grow on each of Farmer Jane's apple trees?

100% -all apples grow on trees!

109) What can you share and still have all for yourself?

Knowledge!

110) I am the son of your grandfather and grandmother, but I'm not your uncle. Who am I?

Your father!

111)   **What has flies and four wheels?**

A garbage truck!

112)   **What can die but never lives?**

A battery!

113)   **What type of a outerwear can you only be put on when it's dripping wet?**

A coat of paint!

114)   **I have branches, but I have no leaves, no trunk, and no fruit. What am I?**

A bank!

115)   **You will find me just once in the morning, then twice every afternoon, but also never in a single evening. What am I?**

The letter "O!"

116) **What has two legs but can't walk?**

A pair of pants!

117) **I live at 423 Daisy Lane in a one-story house that is pink, I mean everything is pink. The people are pink, the dog is pink, the table is pink, the food is pink- everything is pink! And can you guess what color the stairs are?**

There aren't any stairs, it's only a one-story house!

118) **If you cut me with your knife, I won't shed a tear but you probably will. What am I?**

An onion!

119) **I will always be coming, but never arrive now. What am I?**

Tomorrow!

120) **A dad fell off a 30 foot wooden ladder, but he didn't get hurt. How?**

He fell off the bottom rung, only a foot off the ground!

121) **When you use me, you throw me away and take me in when you're done with me. What am I?**

An anchor!

122) **You go to the store and buy me by the yard, but I am worn by the foot. What am I?**

Carpet!

123) **What has 88 teeth, but never brushes them?**

A piano!

124) **Many have heard me, but nobody has seen me. I will not speak unless spoken to. What am I?**

An echo!

125)   **I can be cracked, and I can be played. I can be told, and I can be made. What am I?**

A joke!

One Final Thing...

Thank for making it through to the end of *Fun and Silly Jokes for Kids and Family*, let's hope it tickled your funny, and was able to provide you and your family with all of the entertainment you needed for this rainy day (or sunny afternoon)!

Did You Enjoy the Book?

If you did, please let us know by leaving a review on AMAZON. Review let Amazon know that we are creating quality material for children. Even a few words and ratings would go a long way. We would like to thank you in advance for your time.

If you have any comments, or suggestions for improvement for other books, we would love to hear from and you and can contact us at riddleland@bmccpublishing.com

Your comments are greatly valued and the book have already been revised and improved as a result of helpful suggestions from readers.

Challenge Your Kids
With Some Fun Riddles

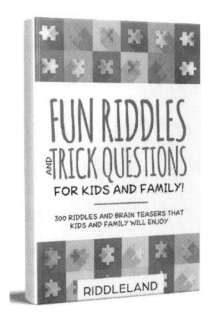

Fun Riddles and Trick Questions for Kids and Family: 300 Riddles and Brain Teasers that Kids and Family Will Enjoy!

This books contains 300 fun riddles and brain teasers of easy to hard difficulty. These brain teasers will challenge the children and their parents to think and stretch their minds.

Bonus Books for the Kids

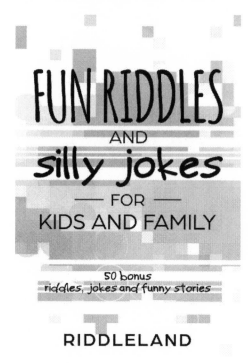

https://forms.aweber.com/form/93/463180293.htm

Thank you for buying this book, We would like to share a special bonus as a token of appreciation. It is collection 50 original jokes, riddles and 2 funny stories

RIDDLES AND JOKES CONTESTS!!

Riddleland is having **2 contests** to see who is the smartest or funniest boys and girls in the world!

1) **Creative and Challenging Riddles**
2) **Tickle Your Funny Bone Contest**

Parents, please email us your child's "Original" Riddle or Joke **and he or she could win a $50 gift card to Amazon.**

Here are the rules:

1) It must be challenging for the riddles and funny for the jokes!
2) It must be 100% Original and not something from the internet! It is easy to find out!
3) You can submit both joke and riddle as they are 2 separate contests.
4) No help from the parents unless they are as funny as you.
5) Winners will be announced via email.
6) Email us at Riddleland@bmccpublishing.com

About the Author

Riddleland is a mom + dad run publishing company. We are passionate about creating fun and innovative books to help children develop their reading skill and fall in love with reading. If you have suggestions for us or want to work with us, shoot us an email at riddleland@bmccpublishing.com

Our favorite family quote

"Creativity is area in which younger people have a tremendous *advantage since they have an endearing habit of always questioning past wisdom and authority." – Bill Hewlett*

Made in the
USA
Middletown, DE